Margaret Nanfuka

LUGANDA - ENGLISH
Phrase Book

GW00585972

Fountain Publishers Ltd.

Fountain Publishers Ltd.
P.O. Box 488,
Kampala, Uganda

ISBN 9970 02 063 3

Printed by *The New Vision* Printing and Publishing Corporation

Contents

ABOUT THIS BOOK

This phrase book is a handy one and will help you to be readily understood on all occasions. It will get you quickly and easily where you want; and what you want. It will also enable you to cope with those minor problems and emergencies that keep coming up now and again.

ACKNOWLEDGEMENT

I would like to thank all those who in one way or another helped to produce this phrase book. I thank Mr. Dick Francis Tumusiime, of *Difra Language Services* who instilled in me the idea of writing this book. I also thank my Luganda teachers for making me what I am, a Lugada teacher in my own right; especially Mr. Fred Masagazi and Mr. Jack Kizza.

1. VOWELS

A - a as in **ant**
E - e as in **e**lephant
I - i as in **i**nk
O - o as in **o**range
U - u as in b**oo**t

For all the consonants, it is just a matter of adding the consonant to the vowel and then pronounce the word e.g. Tata. If you have two similar vowels following each other e.g. **aa** as in sa**a**la then there will be a prolonged pronunciation. *Saala* is pronounced differently from *sala*. The same is true of the following: **seera - sera; siiga - siga**

A wrong pronunciation will give a different meaning. In Luganda the letter *r* is pronounced as the English *l*. e.g. - *Makerere* is pronounced as *Makelele*.

2. PRONOUNS

We have several pronouns in Luganda. Some are written separately, while others are attached to the verb as prefixes which make agreements with the noun.

(a) Self standing pronouns

Nze	-	me	Ffe	-	we/us
Ggwe	-	you	Mmwe	-	you
Ye	-	he	Bo	-	they

(b) Always attached to the verb.

N	-	I	tu	-	we
O	-	You (singular)	mu	-	you (plural)
a	-	he/she	ba	-	they

You will be shown how they operate using:

(a) the verb to be - **okuba - infinitive.**

Ndi	-	I am	tuli	-	we are
Oli	-	You are	muli	-	you are (plural)
ali	-	he is	bali	-	they are

(b) Verb to have   **Okubeera ne**

Nnina	-	I have	tulina	-	we have
Olina	-	You have	mulina	-	you hav (plural)
alina	-	he/she has	balina	-	they hav

Demonstratives

Wano	- here	Kino	-	this (thing)
Awo	- there	Ekyo	-	that (thing)
Wali	- Over there	Kiri	-	that (thing)
				(further away)

Ono	-	this (person)
Oyo	-	that (person)
Oli	-	that (person –further away)

Interrogatives

Ani?	-	who?	: Ani oyo? Who is that?
Ki?	-	what?	: Ki ekyo? What is that?
Kiruwa?	-	which (one)?	: Kiruwa ky'oyagala? Which one do you want?
Lwaki	-	why?	: Lwaki ogenda? Why are you going away?
Ddi	-	when?	: Ogenda ddi? When are you going?
Tya	-	how?	: Ogenda otya? How are you going?
			: Agenda **atya**? How is **she** going?

Wa   -   where?   : Ogenda **wa**? Where
                                  are you going?

Greetings

Greetings in Luganda depend on who you are greeting
and when you last saw him/her. A polite kind of
greeting for someone you see daily would go as
follows: (N.B. You respect this person).

A. Wasuze otyano Ssebo/Nnyabo - Good morning
    Sir/Madam (How was the night).
    Osiibye otyanno Ssebo/Nnyabo -   Good
    afternoon Sir/Madam.
B   Bulungi Ssebo,gwe osiibye otyanno Ssebo/
    Nnyabo?
    Fine, and how are you Sir/Madam?
A. Bulungi Ssebo/Nnyabo   - Fine Sir/Madam
B. Abeeka bali batya? - How is every one at home?
A. Gyebali balungi   - Everybody is fine
B. Weebale emirimu   - Thank you for the work
                          you do.
A. Kale Ssebo /Nnyabi - Okay sir/madam

Of course you may not greet everyone you meet in
town but in rural areas greeting is a rule, and it is very
impolite not to·do so.

Introductions

It's very important for one to know how to introduce oneself.

Nze Peter	-	I am called Peter.
Mbeera Kampala	-	I stay /live in Kampala.
Nnina emyaka kkumi	-	I am ten (years old)
Nsoma	-	I am a student/ I am still studying
Nkola	-	I work
Mbeera ne	-	I stay with....

Some Civilities

Goodbye	-	Weeraba
To more than one person	-	Mweraba
See you again tomorrow	-	Tunaalabagana enkya
Please do me a favour	-	Nnyambaako
Please help me	-	Nyambaako
Thank you	-	Weebale/
To more than one person	-	Mwebale
Thank you very much	-	Weebale/ Mwebale nnyo

Forgive me	-	Nsonyiwa or Munsonyiwe (to more than one person)
Please may I pass	-	Ka nkuyiteko (to one person)
	-	Ka mbayiteko (to many people)

Some common verbs

N.B. When conjugating the verb, remove *'oku'* and replace it with the required pronoun i.e. *n, o, a, tu, mu, ba* (*Example: nkola, okola, akola etc*).

Okugenda	-	to go
Okukola	-	to work
Okusoma	-	to read/study
Okunywa	-	to drink
Okulya	-	to eat
Okutambula	-	to walk
Okuwandiika	-	to write
Okwagala	-	to want/like/ love
Okuseka	-	to laugh
Okukaaba	-	to cry
Okudduka	-	to run

Tenses

In Luganda we have five tenses.
The far past, the near past, the present, the near future and the far future.

Far past	Near past	Present	Near future	Far future
I laughed				
Naseka	Nasese	Nseka	**Nj**akuseka	**Nd**iseka
I went				
Nagenda	Nagenze	Ngenda	**Nj**akugenda	**Nd**igenda
I ran				
Nadduka	Nadduse	Nziruka	**Nj**akudduka	**Nd**idduka
I read				
Nasoma	Nasomye	Nsoma	**Nj**akusoma	**Nd**isoma

You realise that the *n* at the beginning represents the first person singular i.e. *I*. The present and future tenses are easy. Just study them and you will get the idea. The past is tricky. In the far past, words end in *a* and in the near past they end in *e*. There are some changes - for example in the above examples the *k* and *d* of the far past change to *s* and *z* in the near past respectively. This refers to all verbs. There are other changes which are not listed.

3. NUMBERS

1. Emu	4. Nnya	7. Musanvu
2. Bbiri	5. Ttaano	8. Munaana
3. Ssatu	6. Mukaaga	9. Mwenda
10. Kumi	20. Abiri	50. Ataano
11. Kkumi n'emu	21. Abiri mu emu	60. Nkaaga
12. Kkumi n'abbiri	22. Abiri mu bbiri	70. Nsanvu
13. Kkumi n'assatu	30. Asatu	80. Kinaana
14. Kkumi n'annya	31. Asatu mu emu	90. Kyenda
15. Kkumi n'ataano	40. Ana	100. Kikumi
16. Kkumi n'amukaaga	41. Ana mu emu	110. Kikumi mu kumi

As long as you learn how to count from 1 - 10 and 20, 30, 40,.... the rest will be easy.

It's just a matter of joining one number to the other.

4. FOOD

Food	-	Emmere
Water	-	Amazzi
I would like....	-	Njagalayo
One can of....	-	Omukebe gwa ....
One packet of	-	Pakiti ya ....

One box of ....   -   Bokisi ya ....

One kilogram of ....   -   Kilo ya....

Look at the numbers to know the exact amount or number of things you want.

Note: Borrowed words are *Lugandanised*.

Provisions from a General Store (dduuka)

Rice	-	Muceere
Maize (corn) Meal	-	Kawunga ka kasooli
Spaghetti	-	*Supageti* or *Makoloni*
Salt	-	Munnyo
Sugar	-	Sukaali
Curry Powder	-	Bunzaali
Coffee	-	Kaawa
Instant Coffee	-	Use brand name e.g. *Nescafe*
Tea	-	Majaani
Powdered milk	-	Amata g'obuwunga
Margarine	-	Use brand name e.g. *Blue band*
Cooking fat	-	Muzigo or use brand name e.g *Kimbo*
Liquid oil	-	Butto
Omo	-	*Omo*

Match box	-	Kibiriiti
Knife	-	Kambe
Paraffin	-	Palafiini

Some useful words

Raw	-	Mbisi
Ripe	-	Ayengedde
Sweet	-	Ewooma
Sour	-	Ekaawa
Hot	-	Ayokya
Cold	-	Anyogoga
Warm	-	Abuguma

Add: Adjective prefixes depend on the noun class.

At the market

Fruits and vegetables are usually sold by the pile i.e. the seller puts two or more items together. They may also be sold by the item or by weight.

Cabbage	-	Mboga
Passion fruits	-	Butunda
Oranges	-	Micungwa
Potatoes	-	Lumonde
Onions	-	Butungulu

Tomatoes	-	Nyaanya
Carrots	-	Kaloti
Pepper	-	Kaamulali
Egg plant	-	Bbiriŋŋanya
Cassava/Manioc	-	Muwogo
Limes	-	Nniimu
Mangoes	-	Miyembe
Bananas (ripe)	-	Mmenvu
Pineapples	-	Ennaanansi
Sugarcane	-	Kikajjo
How much are these? (price)	-	Bino bya ssente mmeka?
How much is this?	-	Kino kya ssente mmeka?

You can always add the name of the exact item.

At the butcher

Ribs	-	Mbirizi
Leg	-	Kugulu
Tongue	-	Lulimi
Liver	-	Kibumba
Chicken	-	Nkoko
Fish	-	Kyennyanja
Beef	-	Nnyama y'ente
Pork	-	Pork

Goat meat	-	Mbuzi or Nyama ya mbuzi
Is this beef?	-	Eno nnyama ya nte?
This is goat meat	-	Eno nnyama ya mbuzi
I would like beef	-	Njagala ya nte
How much is a kilo of ....?		Kilo ya .... ya mmeka?

At a restaurant

Remember that menu terms differ from one restaurant to another. Don't be surprised therefore when what you order for turns out to be different from what you expected.

I would like	-	Njagalayo....
And also	-	ne
And something else?	-	N'ekirala?
What will you drink?	-	Onoonywa ki?
What will you eat?	-	Onoolya ki?
This has cooled	-	Bino biwoze
The menu	-	menu
Coffee	-	Kaawa
Tea	-	Majaani
Milk	-	Mata
Soda	-	Sooda
Cold soda	-	Sooda anyogoga

What kind of cold soda is there?	-	Sooda ki anyogoga aliyo?
Water	-	Mazzi
Drinking water	-	Mazzi ga kunywa
Passion fruit juice	-	Butunda
Orange juice	-	Micungwa

Some useful phrases

What is there to eat?	-	Mulinayo ki eky'okulya?
We have....	-	Tulinayo....
We have run out of fish	-	Ebyennyanja biweddeyo
I do not eat meat	-	Sirya nnyama
I eat vegetables only	-	Ndya nva ndiirwa zokka
I do not eat fish	-	Sirya byennyanja
How much do I owe?	-	Ommanja mmeka?

Some useful words

Teaspoon	-	Kajiiko
Soupspoon	-	Kijiiko kya supu
Fork	-	Wuuma
Knife	-	Kambe
Plate	-	Sowaani
Glass	-	Giraasi
Cup	-	Kikopo
Platter/tray	-	tule

5.   TIME

Telling the time in Uganda is the exact opposite of what it is in English. So to avoid mistakes which might lead to losses you should learn telling the time in Luganda. The English seven o'clock is *Emu* of Luganda which means *one*.

English	Luganda	English	Luganda
Seven	Emu (1)	One	Musanvu (7)
Eight	Bbiri (2)	Two	Munaana (8)
Nine	Ssatu (3)	Three	Mwenda (9)
Ten	Nnya (4)	Four	Kumi (10)
Eleven	Ttaano (5)	Five	Kkumin'emu (11)
Twelve	Mukaaga (6)	Six	Kkumi na bbiri (12)

Time is said using the word 'ssaawa' e.g. Ssaawa emu - seven o'clock. The Baganda find no reason for saying "eight o'clock" when according to them it is "two" so they say it as it actually is and not the other way round like the English speakers do. The day begins at one o'clock and ends at twelve and so does the night.

What time is it?	-	Saawa mmeka?
What is the date today?	-	Leero mmeka?

6. HEALTH

In the tropics many people suffer from fever. It could be malaria or typhoid and therefore, dangerous so report it immediately. Doctors know English but your landlord/lady or neighbours might not, so you need these phrases and words.

I am ill	-	Ndi mulwadde
I want a doctor	-	Njagala musawo
I can walk	-	Nsobola okutambula
I cannot walk	-	Sisobola kutambula
He/She can't walk	-	Tasobola kutambula
Could you please call a doctor	-	Osobola okumpitira omusawo

All right	-	Kale
The doctor is coming	-	Dokita ajja
The doctor is not there	-	Dokita taliiyo
Show me where the hospital/clinic is	-	Ndaga eddwaliro/ kiliniki gyeriri gyeri
I want a taxi	-	Njagala takisi
I want a Vehicle	-	Njagala mmotoka
Bring drinking water	-	Leeta amazzi g'okunywa
Thank you very much	-	Weebale nnyo
Blood	-	Omusaayi
Water	-	Amazzi

Some useful phrases

I have fever	-	Nnina omusujja
I have diarrhoea	-	Nina ekiddukano
I am vomiting	-	Nsesema
I am coughing	-	Nkolola
I hurt here	=	Wano wannuma
I am swelling inside	-	Wano wazimbye
I hurt here inside	-	Munda wano wannuma
I am in pain	-	Ndi mu bulumi

I feel very hot	-	Mpulira ebbugumu lingi
I feel very cold	-	Mpulira empewo
I am pregnant	-	Nnina olubuto
I am sorry/its unfortunate	-	Ng'olabye
I have a headache	-	Omutwe gunnuma
I have a stomachache	-	Olubuto lunnuma
I have a backache	-	Omugongo gunnuma
My arm is paining	-	Omukono gunnuma
My leg is paining	-	Okugulu kunnuma
My eyes are aching	-	Amaaso gannuma
My neck is aching	-	Ensingo ennuma
My chest is paining	-	Ekifuba kinnuma

(Ekifuba though refers
to both *chest* and *cough*
so specify)

7.   ACCOMMODATION

Most if not all the hotel Staff around can speak
English. If you go to a Lodge or rent a room
somewhere, you might not be lucky to find everyone
an English speaker though you can try your luck first.

Do you have a room for one person?	-	Olina ekisenge eky'omuntu omu?
For two people?	-	Olina ekisenge eky'abantu ababiri?
For three people?	-	Olina ekisenge eky'abantu abasatu?
No there is none	-	Biweddewo
Yes, there is	-	Waliwo
How much is the room	-	Ekisenge kya ssente mmeka?
For one day	-	Olunaku lumu
For a week	-	Wiiki emu
In the room is there a.....	-	Mulimu ....
Shower	-	Sawa
Water tap	-	Ttaapu
Toilet	-	Toyireeti
Bath	-	Ekinaabiro
Fan	-	Faani
Is there hot water?	-	Eriyo amazzi agookya?
At what times?	-	Ku ssaawa ki (mmeka)?
I would like to see the room	-	Ekisenge njagala kukiraba

All right (I'll take it)	-	Kale
I have not liked it	-	Sikisiimye
Is there another?	-	Waliwo ekirala?
Yes - lets go	-	Yee - tugende nkikulage
No, Only this	-	Nedda, kino kyokka
Thanks anyway	-	Weebale
I would like to move to another room	-	Njagala kukyusa kisenge
Why?	-	Lwaki?
Too much noise	-	Kkerere nnyingi
Odour from the kitchen	-	Eby'omufumbiro bimpunyira bubi
Odour from the toilet	-	Toilet ewunya
It's very warm here	-	Muno mulimu ebbugumu lingi
There is no fan	-	Temuli faani
It's very cold	-	Munyogoga or mulimu empewo
The bed is terrible	-	Ekitanda kibi

8.   SOME MORE GRAMMAR
More Verbs

Okusoma	-	to read/study

Okusomesa	-	to teach
Okulwala	-	to fall sick/be sick
Okubeera	-	stay/live
Okulya	-	to eat
Okunywa	-	to drink
Okutegeera	-	to understand
Okubuuza	-	to ask
Okugamba	-	to say/tell
Okwogera	-	to speak
Okutuula	-	to sit
Okuyimirira	-	to stand
Okusaba	-	to ask (for something)/ pray
Okumanya	-	to know
Okuvuga	-	to drive/ride
Okulaba	-	to look/see

In verbs where we have a letter like '*l*' after '*oku*', the verb obtains a letter or two for the 1st person singular and these are fixed between the '*n*' subject pronoun and the verb stem. This is because it would be difficult to pronounce '*nlya*' for example. That's why for okulya, one says '*ndya*' rather than *nlya*.

Formation of negative

Learning how to say something in the negative will require you to learn the negative subject prefixes.

Person	Singular	Plural
1st	si	te**tu**
2nd	to	te**mu**
3rd	ta	te**ba**

You realise that apart from the 't' these negative prefixes have something in common with the positive subject prefixes i. e. *'o'* *'a'* *'tu'* *'mu'* *'ba'*

Examples:

Sigenda Kampala	-	I am not going to Kampala
Tolya mmere	-	(You) don't eat (food)
Tasoma Mmengo	-	She/he doesn't study at Mmengo

Object Pronouns

The following cannot stand on their own but are rather fixed between the subject prefix and the verb - stem. They are:

Person	Singular	Plural
1st	n	tu
2nd	ku	ba
3rd	mu	ba

A**n**ku**ba**	-	He is beating **me**.
Tu**ku**kuba	-	We are beating **you.**
Ba**mu**kuba	-	They are beating **him**.
O**tu**gamba	-	You are telling us or (You tell us - singular)
Mu**ba**buuza	-	(You) ask them.
Ba**ba**gamba	-	They are telling you or they are speaking to you.

OBJECTS:
Examples:

Pencil	-	Ekkalaamu
Book	-	Ekitabo
Newspapers	-	Amawulire
Table	-	Emmeeza
Market	-	Akatale
Shop	-	Edduuka
House	-	Ennyumba
Garden	-	Ennimiro

Plants	-	**E**bimera
Bedroom	-	**E**kisenge
Sitting room	-	**E**ddiiro
Dinning room	-	**E**ddiiro
Town	-	**E**kibuga

Objects always follow the verb. There is no difference between the definite and indefinite article in Luganda though if you need a particular thing where in English you would have said 'the' in Luganda you have to explain what you exactly want.

Example

Give me **the** book (means it is a particular book). In Luganda the article is the first letter '*e*' or '*a*' which is bold in the above examples. The article is always fixed on to the noun.

Alina **e**kitabo	-	He has a book
Agenda mu **K**ibuga	-	He is going to town
Tolya **m**envu	-	(You) don't eat bananas

Prepositions

In	-	mu

on	-	ku
under	-	wansi
infront of	-	mu maaso ga......
behind	-	emabega wa.....
with	-	ne
at	-	ku
up/above	-	waggulu
Atudde ku mmeeza	-	He/she is sitting on/at the table.
Ali mabega w'emmotoka	-	He/She is behind the car.

In a taxi

Who is the conductor?	-	Ani Kondakita?
Where is the driver	-	Duleeva aluwa?
Is this the taxi to Entebbe?	-	Eno ye taxi egenda Entebbe?
Can we get food on the road?	-	Tusobola okufuna emmere ku kkubo?
I don't know	-	Simanyi
I do not think so	-	Sikiwa
Yes (we can)	-	Tusobola

I don't understand	-	Sikitegeera
(I haven't understood)	-	(sitegedde)
Now I understand	-	Kati ntegedde
I am sorry, I didn't mean to	-	Nsonyiwa sigenderedde
Will this taxi pass Kibuli Mosque?	-	Eno taxi eneeyita ku muzikiti gw'e Kibuli?
Where do I get off?	-	Nviiramu wa?
Please tell me when we get there	-	Ombuulira nga tutuuseewo
Not yet	-	tetunaba
Get off here	-	Viiramu wano
Is this the way to....	-	Lino ly'e kkubo eriraga...
Where does this road go to?	-	Lino ekkubo liraga wa?
I am lost	-	Mbuze
I stay at Equatoria Hotel	-	Nsula mu Equatorial Hotel

Over there	-	Wali
In the middle	-	Mu makkati
Drive slowly	-	Vuga mpola mpola
Wait abit	-	Lindako katono
Let's go	-	Tugende
What time do we arrive?	-	Tutuuka ssaawa mmeka?
Is there a vehicle that goes to Jinja?	-	Waliwo emmotoka egenda e Jinja?
What do you want?	-	Oyagala ki?
I want a taxi to go to.......	-	Njagala taxi kugenda
How much (do you charge)?	-	Ssente mmeka?

(Remember that you can always bargain if you have to hire a special taxi)

Could you please reduce	-	Nsaliraako (the amount)
How much do you have?	-	Olina ssente mmeka?
I have........	-	Nnina

| How long does the trip take? | Olugendo lumala bbanga ki? |

Remember that time in English and time in Luganda are six hours different.

Some useful words?

Round trip/return journey	-	Amagenda n'amadda
Now	-	Kati
Left	-	Kkono
Right	-	Ddyo
On the left	-	Ku kono
Stop	-	Yimirira
Go straight ahead	-	Genda butereevu
Down/below	-	Wansi
One way	-	Amagenda
Return	-	Amadda
Watch out	-	Weegendereze
Leave me alone	-	Ndeka
I do not want any	-	Saagala
No thanks	-	Nedda

Go away	-	Genda
Go out	-	Fuluma

If you are ever asking for directions make sure you greet that person first because it would be extremely impolite not to do so.

Time

Day time	-	Misana
Day	-	Lunaku
Night time	-	Kiro
Morning	-	Kumakya
Evening	-	Kawungeezi
Week	-	Wiiki
Month	-	Mwezi
Year	-	Mwaka

Days

In Luganda the days of the week are more or less pronounced as in English. Sunday is the end of the Christians' week and it can be called *Sabiiti*.

Months

The months have their own names in Luganda but they are rarely used. Luganda borrows the English equivalents.

Present, Past and Future

Today	-	Leero
Tomorrow	-	Enkya
Yesterday	-	Jjo
Day after tomorrow	-	Okwosa enkya
Day before yesterday	-	Okwosa jjo
A few days ago	-	Jjuuzi
Tomorrow evening	-	Akawungeezi k'enkya
Tomorrow morning	-	Enkya ku makya
Tonight	-	Ekiro kya leero
This morning	-	Enkya ya leero
Yesterday morning	-	Jjo ku makya
Next week	-	Wiiki ejja
Last week	-	Wiiki eyise
Next month	-	Omwezi ogujja
This month	-	Omwezi guno
Last month	-	Omwezi oguyise
Next year	-	Omwaka ogujja
This year	-	Omwaka guno

Mwezi' also means moon

Later	-	Gye bujja
Long ago	-	Dda nnyo

Everyday	-	Buli lunaku
Always	-	Buli kiseera
Last year	-	Omwaka oguwedde
What day of the week is today ?	-	Leero lunaku ki?
Today is Sunday	-	Leero Sande
What is the date today?	-	Leero ennaku z'omwezi mmeka?
Today is 7th July	-	Leero musanvu omwezi ogwo musanvu
I leave on 2nd October	-	ŋŋenda nga bbiri mu mwezi gwe kumi
I will return after a month	-	Nja kudda nga wayiseewo omwezi

Shops and Market

Always remember to greet the shopkeeper before making your purchase. Most shoppers do not greet but it is rather impolite not do to so. For most of the items in shops, we use the English equivalents, or, the brand name.

The greeting goes:

How are you Sir/Madam	-	**Osiibye otyano Ssebo/Nnyabo:**
I am fine	-	Bulungi Ssebo/ Nnyabo.
Please do you have ....?	-	Olinayo..?
Cigarettes	-	Sigala
Matches	-	Kibiriiti
Eggs	-	Maggi
Butter	-	Butter
Milk	-	Amata
Blue band	-	Blue band
Rubber sandals	-	Sapatu
Soap	-	Sabbuuni
Tooth paste	-	Colgate/Close up (depending on the type you want)
Mirror	-	Ndabirwamu
Razor blade	-	Girita
Sugar	-	Ssukaali

Salt	-	Munnyo
Comb	-	Kisanirizo
Toilet paper	-	Toilet paper
Omo	-	Omo (brand name)
Thread	-	Wuzi
Needle	-	Empiso
Insect spray	-	Insecticide (brand name)
Candles	-	Misubbaawa
Paraffin (Kerosene)	-	Mafuta
Cooking oil	-	Butto

Clothes and Assessories:

Can I help you?	-	Olina kyoyagala? (do you want something)?
No, I am just looking (window shopping)	-	Nedda nkebera bukebezi
I would like	-	Njagalayo
A coat	-	Kkooti
A jacket	-	Jaketi
A cardigan	-	Sweta
A dress	-	Kiteeteeyi

Tight	-	Tayiti
Long	-	Kiwanvu
Short	-	Kimpi
Big	-	Kinene
It does not fit me	-	Tekintuuka
It does not suit me	-	Tekinsaanira
Have you got it in	-	Okirina mu

For colours, you can use the English equivalents though Luganda has its own names for them.

Skirt	-	Sikaati
Night wear	-	Nayiti
This is just what I wanted	-	Kino kye mbadde njagala
How much is it?	-	Ssente meka?
Shoes	-	Engatto
Boots	-	Bbuutu
They are too small	-	Ntono nnyo
They are too big	-	Nnene nnyo
Socks	-	Sitokisi
Bra (Brassiere)	-	Kaleega
Petticoat	-	Peti

Shirt	-	Ssaati
Blouse	-	Bbulawuzi
Trousers	-	Empale empanvu
Shorts	-	Empale ennyimpi
Suit	-	Ssuuti
Tie	-	Ttaayi
Hat	-	Nkofiira

Every day words

Here are some useful adjectives and adverbs. The more of them you learn by heart, the easier you will find it easy to communicate. Due to the fact that we have many noun classes, there are some changes but as long as you have the stem, even with a mistake you will be understood.

If its an adjective for a person the prefix is '*mu*' in singular and '*ba*' in plural. e.g. a beautiful girl - *omuwala mulungi*.

For other objects it keeps on changing.

good/beautiful	-	Kilungi
bad	-	kibi
right	-	kituufu
wrong	-	kikyamu

big	-	kinene
small	-	kitono
hot	-	kyokya
cold	-	kinyogoga
early	-	mangu
late	-	buyise
open	-	waggule
closed	-	waggale
easy	-	kyangu
difficult	-	kizibu
quick	-	mangu
slow	-	mpola
full	-	kijjudde
empty	-	kyereere
heavy	-	kizitowa
light	-	kiwewufu
beautiful	-	mulungi
ugly	-	mubi
old	-	mukadde/ kikadde
young	-	muto
new	-	kipya
clever	-	mugezi
stupid	-	musiru
ill	-	mulwadde

well	-	mulamu (also means 'alive')

Language problems

I don't understand	-	sibitegeera
Do you speak/English?	-	oyogera oluzungu?
Does anyone here speak English	-	wano waliwo ayogera oluzungu/ olungereza?
Please speak more slowly	-	bambi yogera mpola mpola
What does that mean?	-	Ekyo kitegeeza ki?
Could you translate this?	-	Osobola okukivuunula/ okikyusa
Yes, I understand	-	Yee, nkitegedde

Meeting people

I am pleased to meet you	-	Nsanyuse okukulaba
How are you?	-	Osiibye otyano Nnyabo/Ssebo

If you have taken long without seeing a person the greeting you use is *'eradde'*	-	Eradde Ssebo/ Nnyabo?
This is Mr. Musoke	-	Ono Mwami Musoke
This is Mrs. Musoke	-	Ono Mukyala Musoke
This is Miss Namusoke	-	Ano Mukyala Namusoke
How is Anna?	-	Anna ali atya?
Where do you come from?	-	Ova wa?
Where are you coming from?	-	Ova wa?
Would you like?	-	Oyagala?
A drink	-	Ekyokunywa
A cigarette	-	Sigala
Acoffee	-	Kaawa
I am hungry	-	Enjala ennuma
I am thirsty	-	Enyonta ennuma
I am feeling sleepy	-	Otulo tunuma
Sleep!	-	Weebake!
Wake up	-	Zuukuka
See you again	-	Tunaalabagana

9. THE WEATHER

What's the weather going to be like?
Olowooza obudde bugenda kuba butya?

Today	-	Leero
Tomorrow	-	Enkya
this afternoon	-	Olweggulo
Is it going to rain?	-	Enkuba eneetonya?
Is it going to be fine?	-	Obudde bunaaba bulungi?
How long is this weather going to last?	-	Eno embeera y'obudde egenda kumala bbanga ki?
Is the weather going to change?	-	Obudde bunaakyuka?
It's hot	-	ebbugumu lingi
It's cold	-	Empewo nnyingi

It's lovely	-	Obudde bulungi
What terrible weather!	-	Obudde nga bubi
What lovely weather !	-	Obudde nga bulungi

10.   THE HOME
Members of the family

Parents	-	Abazadde
Mother	-	Maama
Father	-	Taata
My brother	-	muganda wange/ mwannyinaze
My sister	-	muganda wange/ mwannyinaze
My cousin	-	muganda wange/ mwannyinaze
Niece	-	mwana wange (my child)
Nephew	-	mwana wange (my child)
Grand father/mother	-	Jjajja omusajja/ omukazi
Brother-in-law	-	Mulamu

Sister-in-law	-	Mulamu
Father-in-law	-	Sezaala
Mother-in-law	-	Nyazaala
Aunt (father's sister)	-	Senga
Aunt (mother's sister)	-	Maama
Uncle (father's brother)	-	Taata
Uncle (mother's brother)	-	Kojja

If your brother/sister is the same sex as you, call him/her *muganda wange*. If the sex is different, call him/her, *mywanyinaze*. Your cousin is regarded as your sister/brother and you call her/him that. Your nephew/niece are regarded as your children and you call them that. Your father's brother is regarded as your father and your mother's sister is regarded as your mother.

11. ROOMS OF THE HOUSE

Sitting Room	-	Ddiiro
Dinning Room	-	Ddiiro
Kitchen	-	Ffumbiro
Bedroom	-	Kisenge (also means room)
Bathroom	-	Kinaabiro
Store	-	Sitoowa
Garage	-	Galagi

12.   FURNITURE

Table	-	Mmeeza
Chair	-	Ntebe
Cupboard	-	Kabada
Stool	-	Situulu
Wardrobe	-	Wooduloopu

13.   HOUSEHOLD EQUIPMENT
Utensils

Saucepan	-	Sefuliya
Cup	-	Kikopo
Plate	-	Sowaani
Saucer	-	Soosi
Dish	-	Disi

Cutlery

Knife	-	Kambe
Spoon	-	Ekijjiiko
Fork	-	Wuuma
Teaspoon	-	Akajjiiko

Others

Door	-	Oluggi
Window	-	Eddirisa
Corridor	-	Olukuubo/ kolido

Radio	-	Leediyo
Television	-	Ttivvi
Carpet	-	Kapeti
Curtain	-	Kaateni
Stove	-	Sitoovu
Charcoal stove	-	Sigiri
Cooker	-	Kuuka

14.   DEATH

Death is a very grave occurance and when someone dies, all the neighbours, friends and relatives come together and mourn the *dead* . It's considered very unfriendly of one who does not got for the mourning. Greet people around first and then express your condolences.

What a pity/it is unfortunate	-	Nga kitalo ba nnyabo/bassebo
What has he/she died of?	-	Afudde ki?
Has he/she been sick for long?	-	Aluddewo nga mulwadde?

What has she been suffering from	-	Yalwala ki.........
Fever	-	Musujja
Headache	-	Mutwe
Stomachache	-	Lubuto
Cough	-	Kifuba
Typhoid	-	Tayifoodi
Malaria	-	Maleriya
He is ill	-	Mulwadde
He has died	-	Afudde
He died	-	Yafa
Mortuary	-	Eggwanika
Tomb	-	*Entaana* - before burial/After burial *Amalaalo*
Grave yard	-	Ekiggya/we baziika
Money offered as condolences	-	Amabugo
Funeral rites	-	Okwabya olumbe

Definitely on such an occasion as burial, you are not expected to be happy when you are greeting people. You do not need to be too smart just wear simple clothes.

15. PARTS OF THE BODY

Head	-	Omutwe
Hair	-	Enviiri
Eyes	-	Amaaso
Ears	-	Amatu
Nose	-	Ennyindo
Mouth	-	Omumwa
Cheeks	-	Amatama
Chin	-	Akalevu
Neck	-	Ensingo
Shoulders	-	Ebibegabega
Arm	-	Omukono
Armpit	-	Enkwawa
Chest	-	Ekifuba
Navel	-	Ekkundi
Fingers	-	Engalo
Breast	-	Ebbeere
Thigh	-	Ekisambi
Knee	-	Evviivi
Leg	-	Okugulu
Foot	-	Ekigere
Toes	-	Obugere

16. PROFESSIONS

Doctor	-	Dokita

Nurse	-	Nansi
Teacher	-	Musomesa
Carpenter	-	Mubazzi
Mechanic	-	Makanika
Farmer	-	Mulimi
Accountant	-	Mubazi wa bitabo
Politician	-	Munnabyabufuzi
He works in a	-	Akola mu.......
Bank	-	Bbanka
Shop	-	Dduuka
Hospital	-	Ddwaliro
Garage	-	Galagi
Library	-	Layibulale (library)
School	-	Ssomero
At the Airport	-	Ku kisaawe ky'ennyonnyi
Store	-	Store
Ministry	-	Minisitule

17. EDUCATION

Teacher	-	Musomesa
Teaching	-	Okusomesa
Studying/Reading	-	Okusoma
A building	-	Ekizimbe

Blackboard	-	Olubaawo
Chalk	-	Ennoni
Book	-	Ekitabo
Pen	-	Peenu/bayiro
Pencil	-	Ekkalaamu (enkalu)
Paper	-	Olupapula
Term	-	Ttaamu
First term	-	Ttaamu esooka
Second term	-	Ttaamu eyookubiri
Third term	-	Ttaamu eyookusatu
Student	-	Omuyizi
Course	-	Koosi

When you want to refer to any subject taught in a school, you can use the English name for it. You will be understood.

The child/student has not paid his/her school fees	-	Omwana tanasasula fiizi
I will pay it	-	Nja kuzisasula
This week	-	Mu wiiki eno
Next month	-	Mu mwezi ogujja
He does not attend classes	-	Tasoma

He escapes from
school   -   Atoloka

Uganda is endowed with so many geographical features. As you move around you might come across these:

River	-	Omugga
Lake	-	Ennyanja
Mountain	-	Olusozi
Hill	-	Akasozi
Valley	-	Ekiwonvu
Stream	-	Akagga
Well	-	Oluzzi
Borehole	-	Nayikondo
Desert	-	Eddungu
Papyrus swamp	-	Ekitoogo
Forest	-	Ekibira

8. INFORMATION

News	-	Amawulire
Newspaper	-	Olupapula lw'amawulire or amawulire
Announcements	-	Ebirango

Radio	-	Leediyo
Daily	-	Buli lunaku
Weekly	-	Buli wiiki
Bi-weekly	-	Emirundi ebiri mu wiiki
Television	-	Ttivvi
Programme	-	Pulogulaamu
News Reader	-	Omusomi w'amawulire
Announcer	-	Omulanzi
Here is the news	-	Amawulire gaagano

19. DAILY PHRASES

In a taxi

Give me some money	-	Mumpeereze ku ssente
At the stage	-	Ku siteegi
Driver let's go	-	Duleeva tugende ssebo!
I am getting off here	-	Nviiramu wano
Extend	-	Musembereeyo/ Mwenyigeemu!
Do not mind	-	Tofaayo
I am coming back	-	Nkomawo

That one is crazy	-	Oyo mulálu
Are you crazy?	-	Oli mulalu?

Hopefully you have learnt enough Luganda from this book to keep you moving. There are some complications though and there are some things I have excluded intentionally.

Luganda has 23 noun classes and this makes it hard for foreigners who learn it to speak it perfectly except with a lot of effort. I will show you how different noun classes make words using the adjective *good - lungi*

Stem : *Lungi*

The book is good	-	E**kita**bo **ki**rungi
The boy is good	-	O**mule**nzi **mu**lungi
The telephone is good	-	Essimu **nn**ungi
The boys are good	-	A**bale**nzi **ba**lungi

As long as you know the stem, you will be understood even when you make a mistake, so do not worry about when to say what. *'It'* in luganda depends on the object you are referring to, again depending on the noun class.

Example

It *(dog)* is eating	-	**Erya (Embwa)**
It *(book)* is here	-	**Kiri wano (Ekitabo)**
It *(telephone)* is ringing	-	**Evuga (Essimu)**
It *(tree)* is tall	-	**Muwanvu (Omuti)**

In order to avoid mistakes, better use the noun/object so that one understands what you are talking about.